Thinking Critically:
Euthanasia

Andrea C. Nakaya

ReferencePoint
Press®

San Diego, CA

© 2015 ReferencePoint Press, Inc.
Printed in the United States

For more information, contact:
ReferencePoint Press, Inc.
PO Box 27779
San Diego, CA 92198
www.ReferencePointPress.com

Picture Credits:
Thinkstock Images: 9
Maury Aaseng: 15, 22, 29, 34, 41, 46, 53, 59

LIBRARY OF CONGRESS CATALOGING-IN-PUBLICATION DATA

Nakaya, Andrea C., 1976-
  Thinking critically: Euthanasia / by Andrea C. Nakaya.
    pages cm. -- (Thinking critically series)
  Audience: Grade 9 to 12.
  Includes bibliographical references and index.
  ISBN-13: 978-1-60152-680-9 (hardback)
  ISBN-10: 1-60152-680-6 (hardback)
  1. Euthanasia. 2. Assisted suicide. 3. Medical ethics. I. Title. II. Title: Euthanasia.
  R726.N355 2014
  179.7--dc23
                                                          2013050177

Contents

Foreword

"Literacy is the most basic currency of the knowledge economy we're living in today." Barack Obama (at the time a senator from Illinois) spoke these words during a 2005 speech before the American Library Association. One question raised by this statement is: What does it mean to be a literate person in the twenty-first century?

E.D. Hirsch Jr., author of *Cultural Literacy: What Every American Needs to Know*, answers the question this way: "To be culturally literate is to possess the basic information needed to thrive in the modern world. The breadth of the information is great, extending over the major domains of human activity from sports to science."

But literacy in the twenty-first century goes beyond the accumulation of knowledge gained through study and experience and expanded over time. Now more than ever literacy requires the ability to sift through and evaluate vast amounts of information and, as the authors of the Common Core State Standards state, to "demonstrate the cogent reasoning and use of evidence that is essential to both private deliberation and responsible citizenship in a democratic republic."

The Thinking Critically series challenges students to become discerning readers, to think independently, and to engage and develop their skills as critical thinkers. Through a narrative-driven, pro/con format, the series introduces students to the complex issues that dominate public discourse—topics such as gun control and violence, social networking, and medical marijuana. All chapters revolve around a single, pointed question such as Can Stronger Gun Control Measures Prevent Mass Shootings?, or Does Social Networking Benefit Society?, or Should Medical Marijuana Be Legalized? This inquiry-based approach introduces student researchers to core issues and concerns on a given topic. Each chapter includes one part that argues the affirmative and one part that argues the negative—all written by a single author. With the single-author format the predominant arguments for and against an issue can be synthesized into clear, accessible discussions supported by details and evidence including relevant facts, direct quotes, current examples, and statistical illustrations. All volumes include focus questions to guide students as they read each pro/con discussion, a list of key facts, and an annotated list of related organizations and websites for conducting further research.

The authors of the Common Core State Standards have set out the particular qualities that a literate person in the twenty-first century must have. These include the ability to think independently, establish a base of knowledge across a wide range of subjects, engage in open-minded but discerning reading and listening, know how to use and evaluate evidence, and appreciate and understand diverse perspectives. The new Thinking Critically series supports these goals by providing a solid introduction to the study of pro/con issues.

Euthanasia

On February 11, 2013, ninety-three-year-old Joseph Yourshaw of Pennsylvania died in his home after swallowing an unusually large amount of morphine (a drug used to relieve pain that can also cause death in large doses). His daughter Barbara Mancini, who had been with him at the time, was charged with a felony for assisting in his death. According to police captain Steve Durkin, "She told me that her father wanted to die and she gave him the morphine."[1] Yourshaw had been terminally ill and in pain, and he had reportedly expressed the desire to end his life. In Pennsylvania, however—as in most parts of the United States and the world—even if a person desires it, mercy killing, or euthanasia, is against the law. Yet despite the law, many critics believe euthanasia is the best option for some people, particularly those who are terminally ill and in severe pain like Yourshaw. Others insist that allowing euthanasia is unethical and will lead to a multitude of problems in society.

Deliberately Ending a Life

The word *euthanasia* comes from the Greek for "the good death," and it is generally understood as taking deliberate action to end a life, usually to relieve incurable suffering. Euthanasia can be voluntary, in which the person dying is mentally competent and has requested death. For example, a terminally ill cancer patient who is in great pain might ask a doctor to administer a lethal dose of medication in order to end his or her suffering. It can also be involuntary, in which death is caused without out a patient's clear understanding and agreement. The euthanasia of a person in a coma with permanent brain damage is an example of involuntary euthanasia because he or she is unconscious and unable to consent. Physician-assisted suicide (PAS) is a form of euthanasia in which a physician assists in the death of a patient, usually by providing a lethal dose of medicine.

Euthanasia is sometimes an obvious act, such as when a lethal dose of medicine is administered or a doctor withdraws life support from a patient in a coma. However, it is not always clear whether certain actions are medical treatment or euthanasia. For example, a doctor may provide a terminally ill patient with high doses of medicine, such as morphine, with the stated intention of relieving pain but with the knowledge that a side effect may also be the hastening of death.

Discontinuing Treatment

One form of intentional euthanasia is when medical professionals withdraw the treatment that is keeping a sick person alive. Sometimes patients remain alive only with the aid of a machine such as a ventilator, which enables them to breathe, or through the supply of food and water through a feeding tube. Withdrawing these treatments can cause death. For example, people with severe dementia often lose the ability to swallow and must receive food and water through a feeding tube. Withdrawing the feeding tube that keeps them alive is a form of euthanasia.

Doctors sometimes euthanize patients in a persistent vegetative state (PVS) by withdrawing treatment. These people have suffered a severe brain injury and appear to be completely unresponsive to their surroundings. They often require a feeding tube and a ventilator in order to remain alive. Although doctors do not know for sure whether PVS patients have any awareness, in most cases they do not recover, and the decision is sometimes made to end their lives by withdrawing treatment.

Sometimes this action is taken with the agreement of family members but sometimes family members oppose the removal of life support in the hope that the patient will eventually recover. The latter scenario occurred in December 2013, capturing public attention and prompting a new round of debate about the ethics of involuntary euthanasia. The case involved thirteen-year-old Jahi McMath of Oakland, California.

Jahi had suffered cardiac arrest and other complications shortly after undergoing surgery to treat sleep apnea. She was placed on a ventilator to help her breathe. According to news reports, hospital officials sought to remove the ventilator after she was deemed brain-dead by two hospital physicians and several outside doctors requested by the family. The family fought the hospital decision to disconnect the ventilator. After seeking assistance from the courts, Jahi was released to her mother and moved to an undisclosed location in January 2014.

End-of-Life Care

To avoid the possible situation of being in a coma, with other people making decisions about their treatment, some people state their end-of-life wishes in legal documents. Then, if they somehow become unconscious or incompetent, doctors will still know how they wish to be treated. A do-not-resuscitate (DNR) order directs medical professionals not to attempt resuscitation if a patient is in danger of dying. For example, if they stop breathing, doctors should not perform CPR. Some patients sign a DNR order when they are terminally ill and suffering; they would prefer to die naturally rather than have medical professionals keep them alive as long as possible. An advance directive is a legal document that outlines a person's preferences for end-of-life care. In the event that the person is unable to express his or her wishes, the directive states whether he or she would like to be placed on a ventilator or kept alive with a feeding tube, among other considerations.

When a person becomes severely ill, such as with a terminal illness, he or she typically receives palliative care. This is a treatment that helps to relieve and prevent the pain and suffering of sick patients and eases the end of their lives. Palliative care can take place at home or in a hospital, nursing home, or other facility. Although palliative care usually focuses on helping patients remain comfortable at the end of their lives, research shows that many palliative care providers also help sick people end their lives. A palliative care provider might do this by giving the patient strong narcotics to relieve pain, knowing that these drugs will also hasten death.

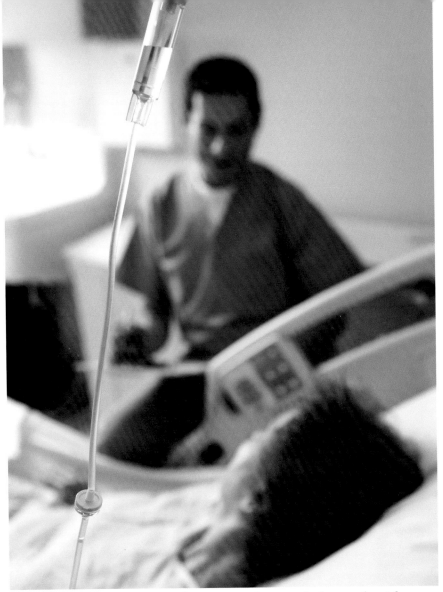

Euthanasia and assisted suicide are most often sought by people with terminal cancer. The loss of control over one's life and loss of personal dignity are concerns that weigh heavily on those contemplating euthanasia.

Controversy and the Law

Even though people may desire euthanasia and doctors may believe it is the best course of action in some cases, it is a highly controversial subject. To legalize it means that a society is allowing and regulating the intentional killing of human beings by doctors or other individuals. Many people insist that this contradicts the mission of medical professionals to protect life and breaks a basic rule of society that prohibits killing another person. Thus, euthanasia is the subject of intense debate and legally is allowed in only a few locations.

Euthanasia is legal in the Netherlands, Belgium, Luxembourg, and Colombia, and assisted suicide is allowed in Switzerland. In the United States PAS is legally allowed in Oregon, Washington, Montana, and Vermont. All locations require that euthanasia cases be reported to a committee or other official body for review. In Switzerland the law does not require that the assisted suicide be performed by a medical doctor, or that the person dying be a Swiss national. Thus, some foreigners travel there for assisted suicide when they are unable to receive it in their own country. Belgium, the Netherlands, and Switzerland are the only places that allow for euthanasia of people who are not terminally ill.

Why Do People Choose Euthanasia?

Official records show that most people who choose euthanasia or assisted suicide have terminal cancer. The Netherlands Ministry of Foreign Affairs reports that patients with terminal cancer account for almost 90 percent of euthanasia cases. Two US states report that a majority of their euthanasia cases also involve people with cancer. Of euthanasia deaths that occurred in Oregon in 2012, the Oregon Public Health Division reported that 75.3 percent of the people had cancer. In Washington the percentage was 73.

Surveys of those people choosing euthanasia or assisted suicide also show that a large percentage are concerned with losing their autonomy and dignity; they would rather end their lives before they reach the point where that happens. For example, many terminally ill people end up unable to bathe themselves or even use the bathroom without help, and they feel that this threatens their dignity. In more serious cases, they may be hooked up to life support and unable to even express their own wishes about their care, meaning that they no longer have control over their lives.

Why Do People Oppose Euthanasia?

One of the main reasons people oppose euthanasia is the threat of something called the slippery slope. Their fear is that once euthanasia is made legal, society will gradually become more and more tolerant of who can and should be euthanized. This would lead down a slippery slope toward an ever-expanding definition of acceptable circumstances for the act of euthanasia. Sliding down this slope could eventually lead to abuses such as euthanizing people with disabilities or coercing elderly people to die.

Others, however, contend that such fears are greatly exaggerated. In the countries and states where euthanasia is legal, it is usually accompanied by strict limits and regulations. As the *Economist* newspaper notes, "For all the limited measures [to allow euthanasia] introduced so far, safeguards abound and evidence of abuse is scant."[2]

An Increasingly Important Topic

As medical advances continue to prolong human life and change the way people die, debates over euthanasia are becoming increasingly relevant to society. According to ethics expert Thomas R. McCormick, the average life expectancy in 1900 was only 48 years, and most deaths were fairly quick as the result of accidents or infections for which there was no treatment. In contrast, he says, in the twenty-first century life expectancy has increased to 77.9 years. This change in life expectancy, which has resulted from new medicines and life-extending medical equipment, has also changed the way many people spend the end of their lives. McCormick says, "With the development of interventions such as ventilators and the subsequent rise of intensive care, more lives were prolonged and an increasing number of seriously ill patients spent their last days in hospital or in an intensive care unit."[3]

Many people do not want themselves or their loved ones subjected to invasive and uncomfortable medical treatment or to spend the end of their lives in the hospital or attached to life-support machines. They believe that euthanasia is sometimes a better option. There continues to be intense public debate over the ethics of this controversial practice.

Chapter One

Can Voluntary Euthanasia Ever Be Justified?

Voluntary Euthanasia Can Be Justified

- Whether to end one's life should be a matter of personal choice.
- The freedom to choose euthanasia makes people less fearful about dying.
- Euthanasia allows people to die with dignity.
- Euthanasia can prevent the suffering of friends and family.

The Debate at a Glance

Voluntary Euthanasia Is Never Justified

- Intentionally ending a life is morally wrong.
- Personal freedom should not extend as far as the choice to end one's life.
- Allowing voluntary euthanasia will make some people feel pressured to choose it.
- Rather than allowing euthanasia, society needs to address depression as well as problems with the medical system.

Voluntary Euthanasia Can Be Justified

"The right to die should be a matter of personal choice. . . . Whether you have a terminal illness or whether you're elderly, you should have a choice about what happens to you."

—Michael Irwin is a retired doctor and the coordinator of the Society for Old Age Rational Suicide.

Michael Irwin, "Euthanasia: The Right to Die Should Be a Matter of Personal Choice," *Daily Mirror*, August 19, 2013. www.mirror.co.uk.

Consider these questions as you read:

1. How persuasive is the argument that every person should have the right to make the decision about how he or she dies? Which arguments provide the strongest support for this perspective, and why?
2. Can you think of an example where the right of one person to die might conflict with the rights of others? Explain.
3. Do you agree with the argument that euthanasia is ethical because it makes the dying process easier for friends and family? Why or why not?

Editor's note: The discussion that follows presents common arguments made in support of this perspective, reinforced by facts, quotes, and examples taken from various sources.

Identical Belgian twins Marc and Eddy Verbessem were born deaf. The brothers lived together and were only able to communicate with one another and their family through a special sign language they developed. In addition to being deaf, the twins developed other serious health problems, including a genetic condition that would eventually cause them to lose their sight. According to news reports, they were experiencing a high level of mental and physical pain that was making their lives unbearable. In 2012, at the age of forty-three and with the acceptance

13

of their parents and the agreement of their doctor, they were euthanized. The Verbessem twins were unusual, but the desire to end extreme mental and physical anguish is a sentiment shared by others. For people like this, whose suffering makes life intolerable, voluntary euthanasia is justified as a way to end that suffering.

The Right to Autonomy

Autonomy, or the right to make decisions about one's own life, is a basic human right. Individuals should be allowed to determine their own fate, and this includes the right to choose death. Debbie Purdy has primary progressive multiple sclerosis, an incurable nervous system disease that causes gradually worsening symptoms, such as difficulty walking and bladder and bowel problems. She is an activist for assisted dying and insists that decisions about ending one's life belong to the individual, not society as a whole. She argues that individuals have the right to make their own decisions about their lives, even if society does not agree with them. "We don't have to agree with the choices people make," she says, however, "we should not prohibit choices just because we wouldn't make them."[4]

> "We should not prohibit choices just because we wouldn't make them."[4]
>
> —Debbie Purdy has primary progressive multiple sclerosis and is an activist for PAS.

Having the freedom to choose euthanasia takes away a substantial amount of fear from dying patients. Just knowing that one has this choice is often enough to relieve fear and sometimes even suffering. Gerda Windgasse, a seventy-two-year-old Belgian woman with a mild case of Alzheimer's disease, does not want to continue living when she she can no longer recognize her family. Windgasse says that when she decides she has deteriorated enough, she plans to receive a lethal injection from her doctor. She describes the way she felt after she made this decision: "When I found a doctor who could help me with euthanasia, tears came down, I was so happy." She says that just having that option "makes me feel free, like I can fly."[5] Knowing that they do not have to slowly deteriorate and lose their mental capacity makes patients like Windgasse less fearful and better able to handle their illness.

Desire for Death with Dignity Fuels Support for Voluntary Euthanasia

People in Washington who chose to end their lives under the state's Death with Dignity Act cited as their biggest concerns loss of autonomy and dignity and the inability to engage in activities that make life enjoyable. While this law specifically refers to physician-assisted suicide, these concerns are similar to those expressed in support of all forms of voluntary euthanasia.

End of Life Concerns of Participants of the Death with Dignity Act Who Have Died

End of Life Concerns	2012		2011	
	Number	(%)	Number	(%)
Losing autonomy	94	94	79	87
Less able to engage in activities making life enjoyable	90	90	81	89
Loss of dignity	84	84	72	79
Losing control of bodily functions	56	56	52	57
Burden on family, friends/caregivers	63	63	49	54
Inadequate pain control or concern about it	33	33	35	38
Financial implications of treatment	5	5	4	4

Source: Washington State Department of Health, "Washington State Department of Health 2012 Death and Dignity Act Report: Executive Summary," 2013. www.doh.wa.gov.

Research shows that patients may be put at ease just knowing that euthanasia is an option, even if they never actually take that step. According to Timothy E. Quill, the director of the Center for Ethics, Humanities, and Palliative Care, data reveals that although most people want to talk about their options, very few actually choose euthanasia. He says,

"One in six terminally ill Oregonians talk to their families about the possibility of an assisted death, while one in fifty talk to their physician, and only one in one thousand actually die using the Oregon Death with Dignity Act."[6]

The Netherlands Ministry of Foreign Affairs also reports that many people who discuss euthanasia with their doctors get enough relief just by talking about it. It says, "Experience shows that many patients find sufficient peace of mind in the knowledge that the doctor is prepared to perform euthanasia and that they ultimately die a natural death."[7]

Dying with Dignity

For those people who ultimately choose to end their lives through euthanasia, it allows them to die a more comfortable and dignified death. Euthanasia advocate Richard N. Côté points out that most terminally ill people spend their final days in a hospital, where doctors use medicine and life-support machines to keep them alive as long as possible. Such an experience is often lonely, expensive, and painful. In contrast, choosing euthanasia allows people to be more in control of what end-of-life measures are taken, if any. For example, many people choose to die at home, and they do it before their illness causes them severe pain. Côté says, "For many, this is a welcome contrast to enduring a lingering, painful, and expensive death in a hospital, connected to often-futile life-support machines after days, weeks, or months of being probed and prodded by strangers."[8]

> "For many [euthanasia] is a welcome contrast to enduring a lingering, painful, and expensive death in a hospital, connected to often-futile life-support machines after days, weeks, or months of being probed and prodded by strangers."[8]
>
> —Richard N. Côté is a euthanasia advocate.

In 2010 Kathleen Carter of North Vancouver, British Columbia, traveled to the Dignitas clinic in Switzerland for a comfortable and dignified death experience. Carter was eighty-nine years old and almost completely paralyzed by spinal stenosis, a disease that causes severe pain and weakness or numbness as the spinal canal compresses. She did not want to die in a hospital bed, with others attending to all her needs. Instead, she and her family spent the end of her life in a comfortable, apartment-like room at Dignitas. She received a sedative to settle her stomach, then thirty minutes later she sat on the couch with her family hugging her and drank a sodium pentobarbital solution. Soon after that she fell asleep and died. In a 2011 interview her daughter Lee Carter explained that assisted suicide was a very positive experience for both her mother and the family. "It was definitely the right thing to do,"[9] she says.

Preventing Loved Ones from Suffering

As Carter's story illustrates, not only does euthanasia allow the patient to die a comfortable and dignified death, but it also can make the dying process easier for friends and family. Terminal illnesses often lead to extensive periods of pain for the patient and extreme stress for loved ones. In an online forum about euthanasia, one respondent explains how difficult his brother's incurable illness is for him:

> For 13 years I have watched my brother go from all star high school athlete and punk rock bad ass to a child like 30 year old. He doesn't always remember me. He is physically unable to eat even though that's all he wants is just to taste something. Most of the time he isn't strong enough to walk or speak, and lacks the motor control to do so consistently. When he can speak his brain is scrambled and can't choose the proper words. I watch every day as he tries to eat imaginary food, or pillows, or he tells the dog to bake him a cake and gets angry when the dog ignores him. . . . I'm 29 and help my mom every day change my 30 year old brother's diapers.

Like many other people who have experienced life with a severely ill family member, this person strongly believes that euthanasia should be an option. He says, "Yes I believe in euthanasia when there is no other hope.

There is nothing wrong with mercy. What's wrong is forcing patients and family [to] suffer through a living hell for no reason."[10]

Decisions about the end of life are very personal, and different people will make very different choices. As a result, the most ethical policy is to recognize that everybody has different needs and beliefs. People must be allowed the freedom to choose euthanasia if they believe that is the best option for them. Allowing patients this choice helps preserve their autonomy, allows them to die with dignity, and can reduce the suffering of the patient, close friends, and family.

Voluntary Euthanasia Is Never Justified

"Euthanasia is in conflict with basic ethical principles of medical practice."

—The World Medical Association is an international organization that represents physicians.

World Medical Association, "WMA Resolution on Euthanasia," April 2013. www.wma.net.

Consider these questions as you read:

1. Do you agree with the argument that a human life is a gift from God and that it is never ethical to intentionally end a life? Why or why not?
2. How strong is the argument that voluntary euthanasia is dangerous because doctors will be pressured to perform it against their will? Explain your answer.
3. How persuasive is the argument that voluntary euthanasia is never justified? Which arguments provide the strongest support for this perspective?

Editor's note: The discussion that follows presents common arguments made in support of this perspective, reinforced by facts, quotes, and examples taken from various sources.

Society institutes many rules for the protection of its citizens, and one of the most important of these is a prohibition against killing another human being. Because murder is such a serious offense, convicted murderers in the United States typically receive extremely harsh punishments, such as life sentences in prison. Euthanasia also involves killing another human being, and like murder, it is never justified—not even if a person desires it. Margaret A. Somerville, the founding director of the Centre for Medicine, Ethics, and Law, insists that a prohibition against killing is an important foundation of society and must be upheld in all situations. She says, "We, as a society, need to say powerfully, consistently and unambiguously, that killing each other is wrong."[11] This means never allowing euthanasia, even when it is voluntary.

Intentionally Ending a Life Is Morally Wrong

According to most major religions, intentionally ending a human life—no matter what the circumstances—is morally wrong. As the National Catholic Bioethics Center (NCBC) explains, "Human life is an inviolable gift from God." Like Catholicism, most other religions believe that God gives humans the gift of life, and thus only God has the right to determine when death should occur. The NCBC insists, "Our love of God and His creation should cause us to shun any thought of violating this great gift through suicide or euthanasia."[12] Religious leaders admit that it can be difficult to understand why a person should remain alive when he or she is experiencing great suffering and it might seem that death is a better alternative. Yet even in such situations, people do not have the right to make decisions about ending life.

Autonomy Must Have Limits

The right to determine how to live one's life does not extend to making decisions about how and when to die. In societies like those that exist in the United States, Canada, and other Western countries, autonomy has limits because one person's choices can affect the lives of others. Patrick Lee, who is the John N. and Jamie D. McAleer Chair in Bioethics at Franciscan University of Steubenville, Ohio, points out that some limits on personal freedoms are needed for the good of society as a whole. He states, "Both law and medical practice recognize rightful limits to autonomy." For example, "the law requires drivers to wear seatbelts and motorcyclists to wear helmets. There are laws against prostitution, dueling, and the use of certain addictive drugs. All laws limit liberty or autonomy to some extent."[13]

These limits are a necessary feature of a free society; they prevent one person from harming another. For example, when a driver speeds down a crowded highway, he or she puts other people's lives at risk. Similarly, if society allows some people to choose voluntary euthanasia, others might be harmed. Such harm is not always physical; it can also be psychological. For instance, doctors might be forced to participate in euthanasia, even when they do not agree with it, and could suffer mental distress as a result. A survey reported in *Dutch News* in 2011 provides support for this view. Approximately half of eight hundred family doctors in the Netherlands—where voluntary euthanasia is legal—said they have felt pressured by patients or relatives to carry out euthanasia.

> "We, as a society, need to say powerfully, consistently and unambiguously, that killing each other is wrong."[11]
>
> —Margaret A. Somerville is the founding director of the Centre for Medicine, Ethics, and Law.

Pressure to Die

In addition to putting pressure on doctors to perform euthanasia, allowing voluntary euthanasia might also put pressure on terminally ill, elderly, or disabled people to end their lives. Research shows that in many cases, these individuals feel that they are an emotional or financial burden to their families or to society. For instance, they may feel that the cost of paying for medical treatment imposes a financial strain on their families. Legalizing euthanasia could pressure them into ending their lives so that they would no longer be a burden. Euthanasia opponent Wesley J. Smith has worked with dying people as a hospice volunteer and deliverer of meals to AIDS patients. He argues that sick people are strongly influenced by others. He explains: "People experiencing serious illness are very vulnerable. They are unwell. They are often depressed, scared."[14] As a result of their vulnerability, patients are highly susceptible to the influence of friends, family members, and medical professionals and easily can be pressured into choosing euthanasia when it is a legal option.

Ben Mattlin has lived his entire life with a severe neuromuscular weakness called spinal muscular atrophy. Because of this condition he has never walked or stood or had much use of his hands. He talks about how patients

Voluntary Euthanasia Has Little Support Worldwide

Voluntary euthanasia, regardless of what form it takes, is not legal in most parts of the world. This fact provides strong support for the view that voluntary euthanasia has no justification. Only a few countries (or states, in the case of the United States) allow a doctor to administer a lethal substance to end an ill patient's life at the patient's request or allow a doctor to prescribe a lethal substance so that the patient can end his or her own life.

United States:	Other Countries:
Oregon: Physician-assisted suicide is legal for the terminally ill.	**Netherlands:** Euthanasia is legal.
Washington: Physician-assisted suicide is legal for the terminally ill.	**Belgium:** Euthanasia is legal.
	Luxembourg: Euthanasia is legal.
Vermont: Physician-assisted suicide is legal for the terminally ill.	**Switzerland:** Assisted suicide, not limited to physician-assisted suicide, is legal.
Montana: Physician-assisted suicide is permitted as a result of a Montana Supreme Court ruling.	**Colombia:** Euthanasia is legal.

Source: Bryony Jones and Ivana Kottasová, "Interactive: Euthanasia and the Right to Die Around the World," *CNN*, November 27, 2013. www.cnn.com.

are always influenced by other people: "I've lived so close to death for so long that I know how thin and porous the border between coercion and free choice is, how easy it is for someone to inadvertently influence you to feel devalued and hopeless—to pressure you ever so slightly but decidedly into being 'reasonable,' to unburdening others, to 'letting go.'"[15] Mattlin says that many people believe his quality of life is poor and that he even has been pressured to end his life. But in fact, his life is very important to him. He has a family, a career, and aspirations for the future, and he does not want to die.

Problems with the Medical System

Rather than allowing voluntary euthanasia, society should focus on improving the medical system so that sick people receive adequate care. This would dramatically reduce the desire to choose euthanasia. In the United States a major force driving people to euthanasia is the lack of adequate care for severely ill and dying people. Critics say that dying people face a confusing insurance system, extremely high medical costs, and a shortage of hospice and palliative care. Ira Byock describes what he has seen as a physician: "There is a maze of appointments, irrational insurance hoops, and requirements, and indecipherable bills. I hear patients express embarrassment at becoming a burden to those they love, dread at the prospect of draining their family's savings and shame of being forced into medical bankruptcy." Many people are pressured into euthanasia to avoid these many difficulties imposed by the medical system. Yet Byock insists, "Much of the suffering I see among people with advanced illness is preventable."[16] The solution to the problem is not to legalize euthanasia but rather to fix the medical system that is driving patients to want to end their lives.

> "Most if not all terminally ill patients who express a wish to die meet diagnostic criteria for major depression and other mental conditions."[17]
>
> —Americans United for Life is a law firm and advocacy group that is opposed to euthanasia.

Depression

In addition to improving the medical system, society should also address the problem of depression in sick people. Treating depression would greatly reduce the desire for euthanasia. In many cases, people suffering from serious illnesses request euthanasia because they are depressed. According to the group Americans United for Life, "Most if not all terminally ill patients who express a wish to die meet diagnostic criteria for major depression and other mental conditions." The organization argues that if the depression or other mental condition is treated, most people no longer want to die: "In one study, treatment for depression resulted in the cessation of suicidal ideation (thoughts about or plans to commit suicide) for about 90 percent of the patients."[17]

Euthanasia is morally wrong and harmful to society. It is never justified, even in the name of personal freedom. Instead, society should reduce the desire for euthanasia by improving the medical system and treating depression in sick people.

Chapter Two

Can Involuntary Euthanasia Ever Be Justified?

Involuntary Euthanasia Can Be Justified

- Ending medical treatment may be a better alternative to continuing treatment that causes pointless suffering.
- Involuntary euthanasia is justified for patients in a PVS.
- It is ethical to disconnect a dying patient's feeding tube.
- Euthanasia of severely ill infants can be justified.

The Debate at a Glance

Involuntary Euthanasia Is Never Justified

- People in a PVS are still alive and deserve proper medical care.
- It is unethical to euthanize patients with dementia.
- Euthanasia of infants is never justified.
- Failing to provide food and water is both cruel and unethical.

Involuntary Euthanasia Can Be Justified

"It seems unfair to deny the merciful death they would likely want to those who cannot request it."

—Thomas Ash is a writer and philosopher.

Thomas Ash, "Euthanasia: Its Varieties and Its Justification," *PhilosoFiles*, 2011. www.philosofiles.com.

Consider these questions as you read:

1. Do you agree that in some cases medical treatment simply causes pointless suffering and should be discontinued? Why or why not?

2. How strong is the argument that doctors should discontinue treatment for patients having no quality of life? Explain your answer.

3. Do you think it is possible for doctors to decide with certainty that an infant is so sick that he or she has no chance of recovery? Why or why not?

Editor's note: The discussion that follows presents common arguments made in support of this perspective, reinforced by facts, quotes, and examples taken from various sources.

In 1990 Terri Schiavo went into cardiac arrest in her Florida home and suffered massive brain damage. Doctors eventually diagnosed her as being in a PVS. As the years passed she remained unconscious and unresponsive, kept alive only by a feeding tube. According to doctors, it was very unlikely that she had any consciousness or would recover. As a result, in 1998 her husband, Michael, tried to have the feeding tube removed so that she could die. While her family strongly disagreed, and it was impossible to ask Terri what she wanted, Michael was adamant that she would not wish to be kept alive by artificial means. He even recounted a conversation they had regarding such a scenario: "Her uncle was very disabled. And he lived with his mother. And Terri said to me,

'If I ever become a burden to anybody, don't ever let me live like that.' And I said, 'Okay. And you do the same for me.'"[18] In 2005, after a prolonged legal battle, the tube was finally disconnected and Terri died. Michael, and others who supported her death, insist that even though it was involuntary, it was justified. The Schiavo case illustrates that there are circumstances when involuntary euthanasia is in a patient's best interest.

Suffering and Quality of Life

Extending the life of a dying patient may simply cause pointless suffering, and taking action to let them die sooner is a better alternative. Kristen McConnell, a hospital intensive care nurse, believes that medical professionals are often forced to keep people alive far too long, when there is no hope of their recovery. She has seen countless cases in which keeping dying people alive as long as possible is painful and undignified; she believes this is an extremely undesirable way to end one's life. As McConnell explains, "We [nurses] see the pointless suffering it often causes in patients and families. . . . It is at worst a high tech torture chamber, a taste of hell during a person's last days on earth." In her opinion,

> We are not helping these people by providing intensive care [that keeps them alive]. Instead, we are turning their bodies into grotesque containers, and reducing their lives to a set of numbers monitoring input and output, lab values, and vital signs, which we tweak to keep within normal ranges by adjusting our treatments, during the weeks and days immediately preceding their death. This is the *opposite* of what should be prioritized when a person is known to be nearing the end of their life without the hope of getting well.[19]

Medical professionals should be able to take action that allows people to die when all that stands between them and death is medical technology.

Involuntary euthanasia can be justified as well when a patient has no quality of life. Patients in a PVS have severe brain damage and are unable to respond or communicate. Although they are biologically alive, their quality of life is very poor. Research shows that PVS patients have very little chance of recovery. In such cases it is justified to allow a patient to die by removing life support. As writer Bryan Cones argues, society needs to focus on quality of life rather than simple biological function, and PVS patients appear to have no quality of life. He says, "I certainly would not want to be sustained in a persistent coma with no reasonable hope of recovery for . . . years while doctors test my brain for function. That's not human life for me." Instead, he says, "I would want those who care for me to allow nature to take its course without artificially sustaining my body's function."[20]

Feeding Tubes

One way of causing a patient's death is by disconnecting a feeding tube. When a person becomes so sick that he or she is unable to eat and drink, doctors can insert a feeding tube instead. By using the tube, they are often able to keep a patient alive far longer than otherwise would be possible. But in many cases the tube simply prolongs the natural dying process, making it longer and more painful than necessary. Therefore, it is sometimes beneficial to disconnect the tube and allow the patient to die naturally instead.

> "We are not helping these people by providing intensive care [that keeps them alive]. Instead, we are turning their bodies into grotesque containers."[19]
>
> —Kristen McConnell is a hospital intensive care nurse.

Patients with advanced Alzheimer's disease, for instance, often lose the ability to swallow. This is the normal progression of the disease, and death follows soon after. These patients have severe dementia and are unable to make their own choices about treatment, so choices are left to family and medical professionals. These decision makers often decide to insert a feeding tube, which keeps the patient alive longer. This is counter to many patients' best interests. Instead, doctors should withhold this treatment and allow the patient to die naturally. "It is amazing how long you can keep someone alive," says Leslie Foote, medi-

A Natural Death is Preferable to Extraordinary Measures

Research done by the California HealthCare Foundation found that most people, regardless of race or ethnic background, would rather die naturally than have their lives prolonged through the use of a breathing machine, feeding tube, or other extraordinary measures. This finding confirms the view that involuntary euthanasia, meaning the act of causing death by withholding or discontinuing treatment even when a patient cannot state his or her wishes, is sometimes appropriate.

Question: *If you had an advanced illness, which would you prefer: Doctors and nurses using everything available to attempt to prolong my life (such as a breathing machine or through a feeding tube)—or—dying a natural death if my heart should stop beating or I should stop breathing?*

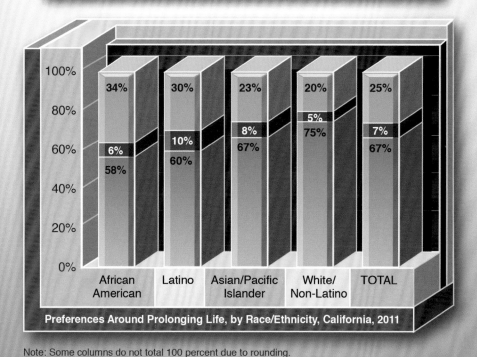

Preferences Around Prolonging Life, by Race/Ethnicity, California, 2011

	African American	Latino	Asian/Pacific Islander	White/Non-Latino	TOTAL
Not sure	34%	30%	23%	20%	25%
Medical providers using everything to prolong life	6%	10%	8%	5%	7%
Dying a natural death if heartbeat or breathing stops	58%	60%	67%	75%	67%

Note: Some columns do not total 100 percent due to rounding.

Legend:
- Not sure
- Medical providers using everything to prolong life
- Dying a natural death if heartbeat or breathing stops

Source: California HealthCare Foundation, "Final Chapter: Californians' Attitudes and Experiences with Death and Dying," February 2012. www.chcf.org.

cal director of the Windsor Gardens Rehabilitation Center in Salinas, California, "but we sure aren't doing them any great favors."[21]

When a person stops eating, the body releases endorphins, which can reduce pain during the dying process. Feeding tubes, however, block the release of these endorphins. In addition, feeding tubes can cause discomfort and infections. Thus, the patient experiences a more painful and drawn-out death as the result of the tube. "Not eating at the end of life is a normal part of the dying process," Foote says. "We have forgotten that."[22] As her comments reveal, even though doctors have the ability to prolong the life of a patient with a feeding tube, it is not always beneficial to do so.

Euthanasia of Infants

Another situation in which involuntary euthanasia can be justified is in the case of extremely sick infants. Sometimes a baby is born with severe medical problems, is experiencing great suffering, and has no hope of recovery. In such a situation, euthanasia may be the best choice. The Netherlands allows this practice. According to the government of the Netherlands, "Children are occasionally born with such serious disorders that termination of life is regarded as the best option."[23] Netherlands law allows doctors to terminate an infant's life if the child is experiencing unbearable suffering, with no prospect of improvement, and the parents consent. Philosopher Peter Singer points out that when infants have severe medical problems, it is not uncommon for doctors and parents to intentionally let them die anyway. Singer argues that it makes more sense to recognize that death is sometimes appropriate and to allow doctors to euthanize sick infants rather than let them suffer. He says that simply waiting for them to die causes more suffering: "[It] seems slow and painful and as I said, terribly emotionally draining on their parents and others." Instead, he argues,

> "Children are occasionally born with such serious disorders that termination of life is regarded as the best option."[23]
>
> —The government of the Netherlands.

"Once you've made that decision [to allow an infant to die], it should be permissible to make sure that baby dies swiftly and humanely. If that's your decision, if your decision is that it's better that the child should not live. It should be possible to ensure that the child dies swiftly and humanely."[24]

Society should not strive to keep people alive when their condition has degenerated to the point of having no quality of life. A civilized society must recognize that there are situations when involuntary euthanasia is justified.

Involuntary Euthanasia Is Never Justified

"There is no such thing as a useless life. . . . A person who cannot walk, or cannot communicate, or is not conscious (as far as we can tell), *still has a right to life and to reasonable measures to sustain life.*"

—Frank Pavone is the national director of Priests for Life, an organization that works to preserve life and is opposed to euthanasia.

Frank Pavone, "Reflections on Euthanasia and Assisted Suicide," Priests for Life. www.priestsforlife.org.

Consider these questions as you read:

1. How strong is the argument that doctors can never know for sure whether another person wants to live or die? Explain.
2. Do you agree with the argument that if doctors do not know a person's wishes, they should not discontinue life support? Why or why not?
3. Do you agree that a feeding tube should always be used in an attempt to extend life? Explain your answer.

Editor's note: The discussion that follows presents common arguments made in support of this perspective, reinforced by facts, quotes, and examples taken from various sources.

In October 2012 California college student and football player Tyler Burton was punched by another man, which caused him to hit his head on the pavement. He was rushed to the hospital, but after a number of surgeries he was still in critical condition. Doctors believed he would not recover and advised his family to consider removing him from life support. According to Burton's stepfather, "The doctor said, 'We have used every tool in the box. There's nothing more we can do for your son.'"[25] Yet just as his family was preparing to let him go, Burton amazed everyone by starting to move. He slowly became alert and began to recognize people. A year later, his family reports that he is able to walk, and that he continues to improve. This story shows the danger of involuntary euthanasia. It reveals that even when a person appears unaware and incapable of recovery, as Burton did, they still have a chance of recovering. Thus, doctors should never end a life prematurely; instead, they should do everything they can to protect every life in their care.

A Persistent Vegetative State

Sometimes a person has an accident or illness that causes him or her to become unconscious; unlike Burton, though, the patient does not recover. Instead, he or she remains in a PVS for years, with no apparent awareness of his or her surroundings. Doctors believe there is very little chance that a PVS patient will ever regain consciousness, and as a result, relatives often request to have the patient removed from life support. Yet science is finding out new information about such patients; research has revealed that they may be much more aware than they appear.

In 2012 Canadian researchers used magnetic resonance imaging (MRI) scans to examine brain activity in thirty-nine-year-old Scott Routley, who has been in a PVS for twelve years due to a car crash. Routley had shown no signs of awareness and was unable to communicate in any way. However, by looking at his brain activity, researchers were able to determine that he is not completely unaware. In fact, scans revealed that he knows his name and where he is, and that he is not in pain. Researchers were able to communicate with Routley by instructing him to think about walking around his house if he wished to answer "yes" to a question, and to think about playing tennis if he wished to answer "no." Each of these thoughts caused a distinct pattern of brain activity that researchers could observe with an MRI machine. According to Adrian Owen, the lead researcher in the study, "Scott has been able to show he has a conscious, thinking mind. We have scanned him several times and his pattern of brain activity shows he is clearly choosing to answer our questions."[26] This study reveals that even when a person like Routley appears to be unaware, he or she may still have significant awareness, and it would be unethical to deny or remove life-saving technology.

Medical Technology Should Be Used to Prolong Life

Family members are sometimes asked to make life and death decisions on behalf of dying loved ones who are too ill to state their preferences. One of these decisions involves the insertion of a feeding tube to supply nutrients to keep the person alive. In a survey of people who have faced this choice, a significant number say they believe they made the right decision when they agreed to the use of a feeding tube to prolong the life of a relative who was dying from dementia.

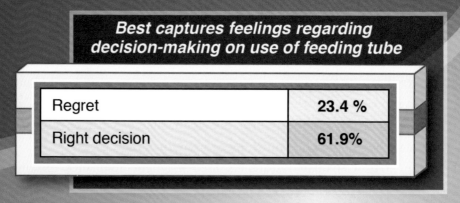

Best captures feelings regarding decision-making on use of feeding tube

Regret	23.4 %
Right decision	61.9%

Source: Joan M. Teno et al., "Decision-Making and Outcomes of Feeding Tube Insertion: A Five-State Study," *Journal of the American Geriatrics Society*, May 2011. http://onlinelibrary.wiley.com.

Patients with Dementia

The idea of euthanizing patients with dementia is equally unjustifiable. As with PVS patients, nobody can know with certainty what is best for a person afflicted with dementia. Writer Paul Donovan's father suffered from dementia, and Donovan insists that it would have been impossible for him or anyone else to make a decision about whether euthanasia was appropriate for his father. He says, "Neither I nor anybody else as far as I am aware knows the cognitive state of the dementia sufferer. They have by the later stages moved off into another world totally. They may be troubled in that place or they may be happy with no responsibilities and simply enjoying life mentally. No one yet knows, so how can any third party make a judgment on another's life."[27]

Donovan agrees that dementia can be difficult for friends and family, but he insists that this is not a reason for euthanasia. He says, "Seeing my Dad go down hill from a strong confident individual to a person that did not recognise his own wife and sons was devastating for the family but what about him? He passed away peacefully, after a good life. A bit of suffering for his nearest and dearest should not really enter the equation on life and death matters."[28]

Euthanasia of Infants

The same can be said for the parents of children who are born with severe, debilitating health problems, with little hope of recovery. When a newborn in this situation is euthanized, it is often done to end the suffering of the parents rather than the infant. This is never justifiable. The problem with infants is that no one really knows how that child's life will play out—whether it is or will be filled with suffering. Joseph Tham, an assistant professor of bioethics at Regina Apostolorum University in Rome, argues that euthanizing an infant is unethical because it is impossible to accurately assess their quality of life. Euthanasia of infants is problematic, he says, "because it is based on somebody else's assessment of a child's quality of life. Since the newborn infant cannot evaluate or define his or her suffering as unbearable, it is usually the physician who makes this assessment and the parents and relatives who give the consent to infanticide."[29]

The case of Nicky Chapman illustrates how predictions about the life of a severely sick infant can be wrong. Chapman was born with *osteogenesis imperfecta*, a rare condition involving brittle bones that fracture very easily. At birth she suffered fifty fractures; doctors believed that her quality of life would be so poor that they suggested letting her die. Her parents, however, ignored this advice and brought her home. Despite only growing to two foot nine, Chapman lived to be forty-eight years old. She

> "Food and drink are a normal aspect of taking care of life and health, not an extraordinary intervention. As aspects of normal care, therefore, they are morally obligatory."[31]
>
> —Frank Pavone is the national director of the organization Priests for Life.

became the first person with a congenital disability to be appointed to the British House of Lords in Parliament. Before her death in 2009, she pointed out that when she was born, doctors said she had "no noticeable mental functions." She said, "That is a little bit different from what I have managed to achieve and where I am today."[30]

Providing Food and Water

Another common situation related to involuntary euthanasia involves feeding tubes. Some sick people, such as advanced Alzheimer's patients or patients in a PVS, lose the ability to swallow and need a feeding tube in order to receive food and water. Sometimes involuntary euthanasia is carried out by not providing that tube or by disconnecting one that is already there. However, this is never justified. As Frank Pavone, the national director of Priests for Life, explains, food and water are a basic human right that should never be denied. He rebuffs critics who argue that feeding tubes are an optional medical intervention; instead, Pavone insists, "When we come back from lunch, we do not say that we just had 'our latest medical treatment.' Food and drink are a normal aspect of taking care of life and health, not an extraordinary intervention. As aspects of normal care, therefore, they are morally obligatory."[31] Withholding this care is unethical.

> "How could dying of thirst possibly be considered a peaceful death?"[32]
>
> —The Patients Rights Council is an organization that works to educate people about euthanasia and assisted suicide.

Denying a patient water actually causes a painful death by dehydration. The Patients Rights Council says that when death occurs in this manner, it is not "'putting them *out* of their misery,' as some would say. Instead it's putting them *into* misery—the misery of dying in an excruciating manner. How could dying of thirst possibly be considered a peaceful death?"[32]

Even when patients have no awareness of their surroundings or appear to be dying, ending a life by discontinuing treatment or removing life support cannot be justified. Instead, doctors should do everything they can to help their patients live.

Chapter Three

Should Physician-Assisted Suicide Be Legal?

Physician-Assisted Suicide Should Be Legal

- Caring for a patient in the best way possible sometimes includes PAS.
- PAS is appropriate when palliative care is not sufficient.
- Legalizing PAS would help patients die with dignity.
- Legalizing PAS would help reduce medical costs.

The Debate at a Glance

Physician-Assisted Suicide Should Not Be Legal

- PAS is not compatible with the role of doctor.
- Legalizing PAS would put unfair pressure on doctors.
- Proper palliative care eliminates the need for PAS.
- A physician should never perform PAS because a diagnosis could be wrong.

Physician-Assisted Suicide Should Be Legal

"I think those who have a terminal illness and are in great pain should have the right to choose to end their lives [through PAS]."

—Stephen Hawking is a famous scientist who is almost completely paralyzed.

Quoted in Reuters, "Stephen Hawking: Assisted Suicide Should Be Option for Terminally Ill," *Huffington Post*, September 17, 2013. www.huffingtonpost.com.

Consider these questions as you read:

1. Do you agree that allowing physicians to perform PAS would not conflict with their role as healers? Why or why not?
2. How strong is the argument that sick patients should be allowed to choose PAS as a way to die with dignity? Explain your answer.
3. Do you think reducing medical costs is a good reason to legalize PAS? Why or why not?

Editor's note: The discussion that follows presents common arguments made in support of this perspective, reinforced by facts, quotes, and examples taken from various sources.

In 1998 American physician Jack Kevorkian used a lethal injection to end the life of fifty-two-year-old Thomas Youk, who was suffering from Lou Gehrig's disease, a debilitating illness that causes weakness and atrophy of muscles throughout the body. Youk had requested Kevorkian's help in dying. This was not the first time Kevorkian had helped somebody die. Kevorkian claimed to have helped approximately 130 ill people end their lives between 1990 and 1998. The 1998 case differed from the others, however, because it led to Kevorkian's conviction on charges of second-degree murder. He was sentenced to ten to twenty-five years in prison. Kevorkian, who died in 2011, never recanted his view that PAS should be legal. In a 2010 interview, he said of his actions, "I have no regrets, none whatsoever."[33]

Many other doctors feel the same way. PAS does not conflict with the role of the physician, which is to help people who are sick and in pain. As difficult as it might be, sometimes that means helping them die. German bioethicist Nikola Biller-Andorno explains that although physicians do generally focus on keeping patients alive, different situations call for different kinds of care. She says,

> The role of physicians is not simply to preserve life but also to apply expertise and skills to help improve their patients' health or alleviate their suffering. The latter includes providing comfort and support to dying patients. Such patients may, after careful consideration, come to the conclusion that in their particular situation, asking a physician for assistance in suicide best reflects their interests and preferences.[34]

In such a case, PAS is compatible with a doctor offering the best possible care.

When Palliative Care Is Not Enough

Even those who are fortunate enough to receive palliative and/or hospice care might desire a physician's help in dying. Palliative care helps relieve and prevent the pain and suffering of ill patients. Hospice is similar but focuses specifically on people who are terminally ill. As beneficial as these forms of care can be, they do not always eliminate the desires of ill patients to control the time and manner of their own death—with a doctor's help. As the Netherlands Ministry of Foreign Affairs states, "Even where patients are receiving palliative care of the highest quality, they may still regard their suffering as unbearable." It adds, "In such cases, euthanasia could represent a dignified conclusion to good palliative care."[35]

One common cause of unbearable suffering is pain. Some people experience high levels of pain that cannot be relieved by palliative care or hospice. For some of these patients, obtaining a physician's assistance in dying is preferable to enduring a slow, painful death in hospice. Timothy E. Quill, the director of the Center for Ethics, Humanities, and Palliative Care, says, "Hospice does an excellent job addressing most suffering for most patients, but there is always a small number of patients whose suffering is severe despite the best efforts of a multidisciplinary team."[36] Quill and others believe that these people should have access to PAS.

In a *New York Times* editorial, Janice Lynch Schuster talks about the death of her grandmother and says that she wishes PAS had been an option. She says, "The end of my grandmother's life proved to be a nightmare when her physicians could not treat her intractable cancer pain." Schuster says, "I would have done anything to end her suffering, but hadn't the means or knowledge. Legal 'aid in dying' might have spared her such overwhelming pain."[37]

> "The role of physicians is not simply to preserve life but also to apply expertise and skills to help improve their patients' health or alleviate their suffering. The latter includes providing comfort and support to dying patients."[34]
>
> —Nikola Biller-Andorno is a German bioethicist.

Death with Dignity

Another reason some seriously ill patients desire PAS is that it allows them to avoid extreme and uncomfortable measures to keep them alive. Some people prefer to die at home, surrounded by friends and family. This is often referred to as death with dignity. Becky Proctor of Boise, Idaho, writes about how her sister chose such a death at the end of her battle with brain cancer. Proctor says, "Most societal, governmental, and religious institutions support and (even require) interventional medical treatment to keep humans alive far beyond what would naturally occur, often just extending the pain and suffering of the terminally ill."[38]

Instead, Proctor says, PAS allowed her to choose the circumstances of her death. With her doctor's help, she died with dignity. According to Proctor, "She died in her home, on her favorite recliner, with her cat on

Americans Strongly Support Physician-Assisted Suicide

Although few states have legalized physician-assisted suicide for terminally ill patients, PAS has strong support among the US population. A 2011 poll reveals that far more people believe that the law should allow physician-assisted suicide than not. Support is especially high among males and people with at least some college education.

"Do you think that law should allow doctors to comply with the wishes of a dying patient in severe distress who asks to have his life ended, or not?"

	Total 2010	Gender		Education		
		Male	Female	H.S. or less	Some college	College grad +
Yes, should allow	58%	61%	55%	50%	66%	61%
No, should not allow	20%	21%	19%	22%	18%	19%
Not sure	22%	18%	26%	28%	16%	19%

Source: Harris Interactive, "Large Majorities Support Doctor Assisted Suicide for Terminally Ill Patients In Great Pain," January 25, 2011. www.harrisinteractive.net.

her lap, her son holding one hand, and her husband holding the other. Just as she wanted."[39] Although not all seriously ill patients would choose this option, it must be a legal alternative for those who wish to avoid a long, drawn-out, and painful death.

Dealing With It Openly

Because of the sensitive nature of PAS, it is understandable that it is the subject of ongoing public discussion. It is important to note, however, that PAS does commonly occur. Yet because it happens secretly, it is difficult to know exactly what is happening and whether any abuses are taking place. By legalizing PAS, society can ensure that it is carried out in an ethical manner. Quill says, "There is an underground practice across the country of physician-assisted death which is not vigorously scrutinized as long as it is kept secret."[40]

> "Hospice does an excellent job addressing most suffering for most patients, but there is always a small number of patients whose suffering is severe despite the best efforts of a multidisciplinary team."[36]
>
> —Timothy E. Quill is the director of the Center for Ethics, Humanities, and Palliative Care.

Quill argues that an examination of data from Oregon—where PAS is legal—reveals that regulation appears to be preventing abuse. Statistics show that most dying people in Oregon are not from groups that might be more likely to be coerced into dying, such as the uneducated, people experiencing uncontrollable pain, or those without medical insurance. According to Quill's review of the data, "97.5% of patients were white, and 98.7% had health insurance. As a group, they tended to be highly educated. Eighty-two percent had cancer, and they all had terminal illnesses." He adds, "Reviewed records demonstrated long battles against their underlying illnesses. Only 2.8% cited financial concerns about treatment as a significant factor in their decision."[41]

Reducing Medical Costs

Yet another reason to allow PAS is that it would help reduce health care costs. The United States spends a huge amount of money on health care. According to a 2013 *Huffington Post* report, it leads the world in health-care spending, and this spending is expected to almost double in the next ten years. Some of this spending is on terminally ill people who do not even want to continue living, yet millions of dollars are spent on their medical care as medical professionals try to extend their lives. If the patients who wished to die were allowed to do so, significant amounts of money could be saved to use on caring for those people who do want to live. Research shows that in the United States a large percentage of health-care costs are spent on the dying. Critics question the logic of forcing these people to live a little longer, incurring huge health-care costs, when they are terminally ill and wish to end their lives. According to a 2012 report by the *Wall Street Journal,* in 2009 a total of 6.6 percent of the people who received hospital care died. However, those 1.6 million people accounted for almost a quarter of total hospital expenditures—22.3 percent.

The reality is that PAS occurs, regardless of whether it is legal, because sometimes it is the best way for a physician to help a dying patient. Legalizing it would help prevent abuse and allow terminally ill people to end their suffering and die a dignified death.

Physician-Assisted Suicide Should Not Be Legal

"Out of respect for life, and out of compassion and care for the elderly, dying, and disabled, PAS should remain illegal."

—Patrick Lee is the John N. and Jamie D. McAleer Chair in Bioethics at Franciscan University of Steubenville, Ohio.

Patrick Lee, "Say No to Physician Assisted Suicide," *Cato Unbound*, December 2012. www.cato-unbound.org.

Consider these questions as you read:

1. Can you think of any situations in which allowing a doctor to perform PAS might influence the way he or she treats a patient? Explain.
2. Do you agree with the author that legalizing PAS would pressure doctors to use it? Why or why not?
3. Taking into account the facts and arguments presented in this discussion, how persuasive is the argument that PAS should not be legal? Which piece of support is the weakest, and which is the strongest?

Editor's note: The discussion that follows presents common arguments made in support of this perspective, reinforced by facts, quotes, and examples taken from various sources.

At their graduation ceremonies, most medical students recite something called the Hippocratic oath. In this famous oath, which is thousands of years old, they promise to uphold a number of professional ethical standards. In the National Institutes of Health version, the oath states, "I will not give a lethal drug to anyone if I am asked to, nor will I advise such a plan." Thus, when a doctor helps a patient die, he or she violates the Hippocratic oath—which is a cornerstone of medical ethics. Making PAS legal clearly violates this oath.

Physicians Should Never Kill

The role of the physician is to heal the sick, not kill them. Researchers J. Donald Boudreau and Margaret A. Somerville insist that assisted suicide is simply not compatible with the role of a doctor and should never be allowed even if a patient's condition is terminal. They argue that

> the art of healing should always remain at the core of the medical practice, and the role of healer involves providing patients with hope and renewed aspirations, however tenuous and temporary. . . . Euthanizing and healing are intrinsically incompatible. Involvement of physicians in such interventions is unethical and harms the fundamental role of the doctor as healer.[42]

Numerous professional medical associations believe that doctors should not be involved in ending a patient's life and therefore strongly oppose euthanasia and PAS. The American Medical Association (AMA) argues that allowing these practices would cause more harm than good. The AMA contends that "euthanasia is fundamentally incompatible with the physician's role as healer, would be difficult or impossible to control, and would pose serious society risks."[43] The association worries that legalizing euthanasia could lead to using it on mentally incompetent people and other vulnerable groups. The World Medical Association urges "all National Medical Associations and physicians to refrain from participating in euthanasia, even if national law allows it."[44]

> "Euthanasia is fundamentally incompatible with the physician's role as healer, would be difficult or impossible to control, and would pose serious society risks."[43]
>
> —The AMA promotes scientific advancement and improved public health.

Putting Pressure on Doctors

PAS not only contradicts the role of the doctor as healer, but it also puts pressure on all doctors to take part in it, even those who do not want to.

Better End-of-Life Care, Not Assisted Suicide, Is Needed

Rather than giving terminally ill patients the means to kill themselves, physicians should focus on providing good, end-of-life (or palliative) care. This would eliminate the need for physician-assisted suicide but, at present, it does not occur often enough. According to a 2010 study of hospitals across the country, between 44.4 and 62.2 percent of Medicare patients with cancer receive hospice care at the end of their lives and even those patients spend very few days in hospice settings.

Hospital Name	City	Percent of cancer patients enrolled in hospice during the last month of life	Hospice days per cancer patient during the last month of life
St. Joseph's Hospital & Medical Center	Phoenix, AZ	67.4	10.9
University of Alabama Hospital	Birmingham, AL	62.2	11.4
Loma Linda University Medical Center	Loma Linda, CA	61.7	9.8
UAMS Medical Center	Little Rock, AR	59.3	10.0
Bridgeport Hospital	Bridgeport, CT	55.3	6.0
University of California Davis Medical Center	Sacramento, CA	53.1	9.5
Stanford Hospital and Clinics	Stanford, CA	52.9	9.0
University Medical Center	Tucson, AZ	50.6	7.0
City of Hope National Medical Center	Duarte, CA	50.2	6.1
UCLA Medical Center	Los Angeles, CA	48.4	6.1
UCSF Medical Center	San Francisco, CA	45.3	7.5
Hartford Hospital	Hartford, CT	44.6	5.8
St. Francis Hospital and Medical Center	Hartford, CT	44.4	6.7
Cedars-Sinai Medical Center	Los Angeles, CA	33.7	4.4

Source: Dartmouth Institute for Health Policy & Clinical Practice, "Quality of End-of-Life Cancer Care for Medicare Beneficiaries: Regional and Hospital-Specific Analysis," November 16, 2010. www.dartmouthatlas.org.

British doctor Chris Lancelot uses the case of abortion in Great Britain to illustrate how this might happen. He points out that when abortion was first legalized there, it was rarely performed and it was easy for doctors to choose not to participate. Lancelot argues, however, that abortion soon became more and more common, and eventually it was an expected part of the job of a doctor. He says, "Within a few years, it became more difficult for conscientious objectors [to abortion] to obtain a job on a gynaecology rotation, or to undertake training in gynaecology, on the grounds that everyone was required to 'share the load of a job none of us likes.'"[45] He worries that if PAS is legalized, it will slowly become such an accepted part of the medical practice that doctors will face very strong pressure to perform it.

The Importance of Palliative Care

Instead of helping terminal patients end their lives, physicians should focus on providing good palliative care to reduce patients' stress and make the end of their lives comfortable. Research shows that many people with terminal illnesses do not receive good care. This could help explain why they seek out PAS. According to a 2011 report by the Center to Advance Palliative Care (CAPC) and the National Palliative Care Research Center (NPCRC), millions of Americans do not have access to palliative care when they need it. The report states that only one palliative care physician is available for every twelve hundred people with a life-threatening or serious illness. It says, "Most people living with a serious illness experience inadequately treated symptoms, fragmented care, poor communication with their doctors and enormous strains on their family caregivers."[46]

The shortage of trained medical professionals and facilities for hospice care is another problem that likely affects the number of people who ask their doctors to help them die. According to Quill, only about 30 percent of dying patients receive hospice care. This problem is expected to worsen because the American population is aging. The report by the CAPC and the NPCRC predicts that the number of Americans living with serious illness is expected to more than double over the next twenty-five years. Without good palliative care, PAS is an attractive alternative for many people. The idea that people want to die because they cannot obtain quality end-of-life care is an abomination, and legalizing PAS will only serve to institutionalize this problem.

Rather than making doctor-assisted suicide legal, civilized societies should develop quality end-of-life care for their citizens. Proper palliative care that addresses pain, depression, and other problems eliminates the need for PAS. Ilora Finlay, a professor of palliative medicine and a member of the British House of Lords, says, "As a palliative care physician I see requests [for PAS] vanish when suffering people get the support they need; many are glad to be living well months or years longer than they believed possible."[47]

The Possibility of Misdiagnosis

This raises another important point, which is that doctors do not always know for certain what course a patient's health will take. Medical diagnoses and prognoses are based on facts and experience. Sometimes, even when they are made in good faith, they turn out to be wrong. With health, there are always exceptions to the general rules. As Massachusetts physician Kerry Pound says, "All health care providers have experienced the desperately ill patient who somehow survives against all odds and the relatively well patient who dies shortly after a diagnosis."[48]

Oregon resident Jeanette Hall has experienced this firsthand. Hall was diagnosed with cancer in 2000 and was told that she had six months to a year to live. She approached her doctor about assisted suicide, but he did not give her that option. "Instead," she says, "he encouraged me to not give up and ultimately I decided to fight the cancer." She adds, "It is now 12 years later. If [he] . . . had believed in assisted suicide, I would be dead."[49] Her doctor agrees that the availability of assisted suicide can cause people to give up too quickly.

> "As a palliative care physician I see requests [for PAS] vanish when suffering people get the support they need; many are glad to be living well months or years longer than they believed possible."[47]
>
> —Ilora Finlay is a professor of palliative medicine and a member of the British House of Lords.

Not Always a "Good Death"

Finally, although many people advocate for PAS because they believe it allows a person to have a good death, evidence shows that a death from PAS can actually be painful and drawn out. Bioethicist Ezekiel J. Emanuel insists that in many cases euthanasia is not actually a good death. He says, "It turns out that many things can go wrong during an assisted suicide. Patients vomit up the pills they take. They don't take enough pills. They wake up instead of dying." According to Emanuel, "Patients in . . . [a] Dutch study vomited up their medications in 7 percent of cases; in 15 percent of cases, patients either did not die or took a very long time to die—hours, even days."[50] Thus, patients who believe they are choosing a quick, painless death through PAS can actually end up experiencing a long, painful one.

PAS is contrary to the role of a doctor and should not be made legal. It puts unfair pressure on doctors and may even lead to the death of patients who could have survived. Instead, health-care professionals should focus on providing positive support and good palliative care for patients.

Chapter Four

Does Allowing Euthanasia Lead to Abuse?

Allowing Euthanasia Leads to Abuse

- Legalization eventually leads to the euthanasia of vulnerable groups in society.
- Europe's experience with euthanasia shows that legalization leads to abuse.
- Euthanasia threatens the disabled.
- If euthanasia is legalized, it could be used to reduce health-care costs.

The Debate at a Glance

Allowing Euthanasia Does Not Lead to Abuse

- Regulation reduces abuse by ensuring that euthanasia happens according to strict guidelines.
- The experiences of the Netherlands and the United States show that legalization does not lead to abuse.
- Legalization might lead to increased permissiveness about who can choose to die, but this does not equal abuse.
- Fears about legalization are based on ignorance.

Allowing Euthanasia Leads to Abuse

"In all jurisdictions [with legalized euthanasia], laws and safeguards were put in place to prevent abuse. . . . These laws and safeguards are regularly ignored and transgressed in all the jurisdictions."

—José Pereira is the medical chief of the palliative care programs at Bruyère Continuing Care and the Ottawa Hospital in Ottawa, Canada.

José Pereira, "Legalizing Euthanasia or Assisted Suicide: The Illusion of Safeguards and Controls, *Current Oncology*, vol. 18, no. 2, 2011. www.current-oncology.com.

Consider these questions as you read:

1. Do you think euthanasia should be legal? Why or why not?
2. Do you agree that disabled people are particularly threatened by the legalization of euthanasia? Explain.
3. Taking into account the facts and ideas presented in this discussion, how persuasive is the argument that euthanasia leads to abuse? Which facts and ideas are strongest, and why?

Editor's note: The discussion that follows presents common arguments made in support of this perspective, reinforced by facts, quotes, and examples taken from various sources.

In 2012, ten years after Belgium legalized euthanasia, the European Institute of Bioethics (EIB) reviewed the country's experience. In its report the EIB expressed concern over what it found. The organization reported that euthanasia in Belgium has become trivialized and less strictly regulated over the years: "Initially legalized under very strict conditions, euthanasia has gradually become a very normal and even ordinary act."[51] In addition, the EIB found indications that there is little government monitoring of euthanasia in Belgium, meaning that the law is likely abused and that such abuse is going unrecognized and unpunished. Belgium's Federal Control and Assessment Commission reviews euthanasia cases after they have occurred and has the ability to forward them to the police for prosecution if it finds that the law has not been followed. Nonetheless, the EIB considered the commission to be an ineffective means of control. It found that of the more than five thousand cases of euthanasia that have been reported since 2002, none has ever been referred for prosecution. In the opinion of the EIB, this means the commission is not doing its job.

Abuse Is Inevitable

As the case of Belgium illustrates, legalizing euthanasia leads to abuse. The gradual normalization of euthanasia can lead to a widening of circumstances when it is considered appropriate. If euthanasia is initially permitted only for the terminally ill, it gradually might find acceptance next for people who are not terminally ill but are in severe pain. Little by little, the acceptable categories continue to expand to include vulnerable groups such as the disabled, children, and the elderly. Euthanasia opponent Wesley J. Smith argues that "the Culture of Death is voracious. Once it begins to feed, it is never satiated, the categories of the killable, never finally enough."[52]

> "Initially legalized under very strict conditions, euthanasia has gradually become a very normal and even ordinary act."[51]
>
> —The EIB works to educate people about bioethics issues.

This fear is backed up by evidence. In 2013 France's national ethics committee examined euthanasia practices in Belgium, Luxembourg, and the Netherlands and found that "these countries legalised euthanasia for patients in the terminal stage who are able to decide for themselves, but in practice the target group has progressively grown broader and been extended to vulnerable groups in society."[53] For example, in some cases the Netherlands allows euthanasia for people who are not able to make an informed decision, such as those with dementia. The committee warns that legalizing euthanasia is dangerous to society because it threatens vulnerable groups.

Legalization Leads to Increasing Deaths

When euthanasia is legal, the number of people choosing to be euthanized steadily increases, as acceptable reasons for euthanasia gradually expand. These charts show that this has been the case in both the Netherlands and Belgium, where there has been a steady increase in euthanasia deaths since legalization in these two countries.

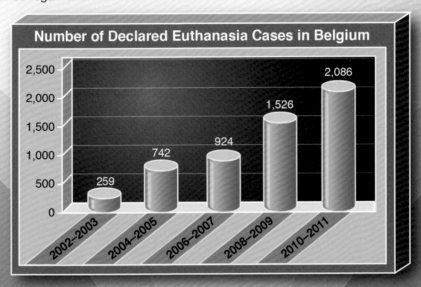

Number of Declared Euthanasia Cases in Belgium

Year	Cases
2002–2003	259
2004–2005	742
2006–2007	924
2008–2009	1,526
2010–2011	2,086

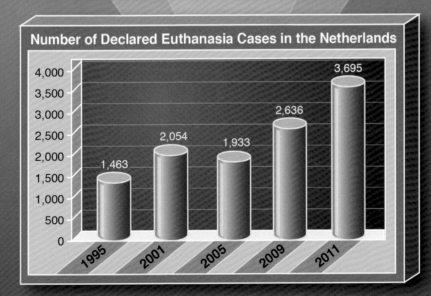

Number of Declared Euthanasia Cases in the Netherlands

Year	Cases
1995	1,463
2001	2,054
2005	1,933
2009	2,636
2011	3,695

Source: Jocelyn Saint-Arnaud, "The Slippery Slope and the Application of Euthanasia Laws in the Netherlands and Belgium," University of Montreal and the Hôpital du Sacré-Cœur de Montréal, April 2013. http://creum.umontreal.ca.

Belgian Tom Mortier agrees that euthanasia in his country has become too easy, with not enough regulation to protect the vulnerable. His mother—who suffered from chronic depression—was euthanized in April 2012 at a hospital in Belgium. Mortier says he was not involved in the decision-making process or even contacted by the doctor who gave his mother the lethal injection. He believes the doctor agreed to euthanasia far too quickly, and that his mother needed help rather than euthanasia. He questions whether his mother was even capable of freely making the choice to die. He says, "Can a mentally ill person make a 'free choice?'" In addition, he says, "Why didn't the doctors try to arrange a meeting between our mother and her children?"[54] Mortier's case illustrates how the medical community might accede to a patient's wishes without even offering or examining alternatives. If euthanasia were illegal, Mortier's mother might have been referred to a psychiatrist who could have evaluated her state of mind, her medications, and her treatment plan rather than allowing her to choose death.

Abuse of the Disabled

Disabled people are particularly concerned about the legalization of euthanasia. Many disabled people have to fight to control their lives and to dispel the perception that they are less valuable than people without disabilities. Some fear that if society legalizes euthanasia, they may be pressured to die.

William J. Peace's story exemplifies this fear. Peace has been paralyzed since 1978 and uses a wheelchair. During one of his hospital experiences while suffering from a severely infected wound, the physician there explained the severity of the situation:

> He grimly told me I would be bedbound for at least six months and most likely a year or more. That there was a good chance the wound would never heal. If this happened, I would never sit in my wheelchair. I would never be able to work again. Not close to done, he told me I was looking at a life of complete and utter dependence. . . . Most people with the type of wound I had ended up in a nursing home.[55]

At this point, according to Peace, the physician offered to help end his life instead. Peace argues that many people, like this doctor, believe that the life of a person with disabilities is not worth living. He says, "My existence as a person with a disability was not valued. Many people—the physician I met that fateful night included—assume disability is a fate worse than death."[56] Disabled people like Peace worry that society's prejudices might lead disabled people into feeling pressured to request or agree to euthanasia.

A Way to Lower Health-Care Costs

Another fear is that legalizing euthanasia will lead to its use as a way to contain health-care costs. Marilyn Golden, a senior policy analyst with the Disability Rights Education & Defense Fund, points out that the health-care industry is highly motivated by cost. She believes that euthanasia might be seen as a dangerously attractive low-cost option. She says, "As the health care industry evolves, cost of care is becoming an increasingly prominent decision point, which in turn prompts more attempts by cost-minded administrators and HMOs to cut these costs however they can."[57]

Golden gives an example of what she believes is a cost-cutting measure in Oregon, which allows assisted suicide. She cites the experience of Barbara Wagner, an Oregon woman who was diagnosed with lung cancer in 2008. Her doctor prescribed treatment with chemotherapy. Golden explains what happened next: "Wagner received a letter from the Oregon state health plan that indicated it would not pay for the treatment prescribed by her doctor; however, they would pay for her assisted suicide."[58] Golden and other critics charge that by making euthanasia easy and alternative sources of treatment more expensive and difficult—as in the case of Wagner—the health-care industry can easily pressure people to choose euthanasia.

> "The Culture of Death is voracious. Once it begins to feed, it is never satiated, the categories of the killable, never finally enough."[52]
>
> —Wesley J. Smith is a lawyer and author who has written numerous articles about euthanasia.

Euthanasia and Organ Donation

The potential for abuse also extends to organ donations. Under the existing organ donation system, the organs of patients who undergo euthanasia are not usually donated. Because of the shortage of organs, however, this practice could be reversed in the future if euthanasia became widespread and legally acceptable. The United States and the world face a serious shortage of transplantable organs. People who choose death through euthanasia could potentially provide much-needed organs. As researchers Dominic Wilkinson and Julian Savulescu point out, "The resources needed to meet the demand for organs are potentially available. Every day there are a large number of patients, who die in controlled circumstances in hospital, whose organs could potentially save the lives of others. But the vast majority of these organs are buried or burned."[59]

This represents a serious threat to patients who might be encouraged to choose euthanasia so that someone else might benefit from their organs. Euthanasia critic Smith worries that harvesting organs from people who choose to die could create an incentive for society to actually encourage euthanasia. This attitude, he contends, "turns a new and dangerous corner by giving the larger society an explicit stake in the deaths of people with seriously disabling or terminal conditions."[60]

Legalizing euthanasia opens the door to many types of abuse, which could include abuse of the disabled and the encouragement of euthanasia to cut health-care costs or increase organ donation. It should not be legalized.

Allowing Euthanasia Does Not Lead to Abuse

"For the limited measures introduced so far, safeguards abound and evidence of abuse is scant."

—The *Economist* is a weekly newspaper.

Economist, "Over My Dead Body: Assisted Suicide," October 20, 2012. www.economist.com.

Consider these questions as you read:

1. Do you agree that legalizing euthanasia or PAS will help reduce abuse? Why or why not?
2. How strong is the argument that increased permissiveness regarding euthanasia does not result in abuse? Explain your answer.
3. Which pieces of evidence in this discussion provide the strongest support for the argument that legalization does not result in abuse? Why do you think they are the strongest?

Editor's note: The discussion that follows presents common arguments made in support of this perspective, reinforced by facts, quotes, and examples taken from various sources.

In 2002 the Netherlands became the first country in the world to pass a law allowing euthanasia. Critics worried that allowing this practice would lead to abuse. A report issued ten years after legalization shows that such fears were unfounded. In the 2012 report, published in the medical journal *Lancet*, researchers investigated euthanasia trends in the Netherlands before and after the enactment of the 2002 law. They did not find any significant indications of abuse due to legalization. For example, they reported that there did not seem to be a disproportionate number of cases in vulnerable groups, such as elderly people. In fact, the researchers found that most cases of euthanasia happened among younger people and cancer patients. In addition, fewer than half of euthanasia requests to physicians were granted, indicating that permission for euthanasia is not simply granted to anyone who asks. The researchers concluded that "in the Netherlands the euthanasia law resulted in a relatively transparent practice."[61] As the case of the Netherlands shows, allowing euthanasia does not lead to abuse.

Regulation Reduces Abuse

In fact, when a government legalizes and regulates euthanasia, as the Netherlands has, it actually reduces abuse. By regulating it, the government can reduce abuse by ensuring that the practice happens according to specific guidelines. There is widespread evidence that euthanasia occurs all over the world—even though it is not legal in most countries. Although it is difficult to determine exactly how common euthanasia is, stories from health-care professionals and friends and families of sick patients reveal that it occurs frequently. In a widely cited study from 1998 published in the *Journal of the American Medical Association*, it was reported that of 355 US oncologists surveyed, 5 percent had performed euthanasia and 5 percent had performed PAS.

> "In the Netherlands the euthanasia law resulted in a relatively transparent practice."[61]
>
> —Bregje D. Onwuteaka-Philipsen is a professor of end-of-life research.

Preventing Abuse in the Netherlands

In a publication about euthanasia, the Netherlands Ministry of Foreign Affairs explains that recognizing this reality is actually one of the reasons that euthanasia has been decriminalized there: "The Dutch government does not want to turn a blind eye to the fact that euthanasia happens." Instead, it says, "The main aim of the [country's euthanasia] policy is to bring matters into the open."[62] In the Netherlands the practice of euthanasia is strictly regulated to prevent abuse. For example, doctors who engage in euthanasia must follow numerous criteria, including consulting

Elderly Are Not at Risk from Legalized Euthanasia

Fears of elderly people being pressured into choosing euthanasia to avoid becoming a burden are not based on fact. In the Netherlands, where euthanasia has been allowed since 2001, the percentage of deaths by age group changed little in the decade after the law's passage.

Age (years)	All deaths in 2010	Euthanasia and physician-assisted suicide		
		2001	2005	2010
0–64	19%	5.0%	3.5%	5.6%
65–79	31%	3.3%	2.1%	4.0%
≥80	51%	1.4%	0.8%	1.4%

Source: Bregje D. Onwuteaka-Philipsen el al., "Trends in End-Of-Life Practices Before and After the Enactment of the Euthanasia Law in the Netherlands from 1990 to 2010: A Repeated Cross-Sectional Survey," *Lancet*, July 11, 2012. www.thelancet.com.

with at least one other doctor with no connection to the case and making sure the patient's request is voluntary and well considered. Doctors must also report euthanasia cases to review committees, which ensure that no violations of the law have occurred.

In addition to the *Lancet* report, other studies also have found that the Netherlands is doing a good job of avoiding euthanasia-related abuse. For example, the 2011 annual report by the Netherlands' regional euthanasia review committees also shows little evidence of abuse. It reports that the committees received 3,695 notifications of termination of life on request in 2011. Of these, the committees report, only four cases were found in which the physician had not acted in accordance with the law.

Oregon and Washington

The experiences of Oregon and Washington offer further confirmation that legalization does not lead to abuse. Physician-assisted suicide has been legal in Oregon since 1994 and in Washington since 2008. In both states, researchers have found little evidence of abuse. For example, some people feared that legalizing the practice would lead to a high number of deaths among vulnerable populations, such as the uninsured, the uneducated, and minorities. In a 2012 report, Gail Van Norman from the University of Washington, Seattle, examined the data to see whether such fears had come true; she found that this has not been the case. According to Van Norman, "In areas where PAS and EU [euthanasia] are practiced legally, there is little evidence at this time to support concerns that the socially vulnerable are being systematically exploited." Instead of patients from vulnerable populations being euthanized, she says, "Most patients were white (95.6 percent), well educated (more than 70 percent with college education), and are insured (96.7 percent). The majority (96.7 percent) were enrolled in hospice care." Overall, she says, "Washington and Oregon residents are likely to be well educated with regard to their end-of-life options."[63]

> "The law in Oregon has been in effect for 14 years, and the evidence is clear that it is used sparingly and exactly as intended."[66]
>
> —Marcia Angell is a senior lecturer in social medicine at Harvard University Medical School.

And in Oregon, according to bioethicist Ezekiel J. Emanuel, the number of people actually taking advantage of PAS has remained relatively small. He says, "In Oregon, between 1998 and 2011, 596 patients used physician-assisted suicide—about 0.2 percent of dying patients in the state."[64] Likewise, the number of people choosing PAS in Washington is also relatively small.

Increased Permissiveness Does Not Mean Abuse

In some places legalization has led to a greater acceptance of euthanasia and an expansion of allowable categories. In the Netherlands, for instance, euthanasia was initially only legal for the terminally ill. It is now allowed for other groups, including those with psychological suffering. This increased permissiveness, however, does not mean that abuse is taking place. Writer David Benatar points out that rather than seeing it as abuse, many people are in favor of the expansion of euthanasia. Those who assume that the expansion of euthanasia in the Netherlands has led to morally questionable cases are mistaken. The Netherlands is increasingly tolerant of who can be euthanized because its population believes that there are people other than the terminally ill who should have the right to choose death. As Benatar explains, "Some of us think that the suffering that a person endures need not be the product of a *terminal* disease in order for it to be intolerable. We also recognize that some mental suffering is intractable and as unbearable as physical suffering."[65] Increased permissiveness can occur without abuse.

Fear of the Unknown

The fear of abuse is often based on lack of knowledge. Because euthanasia is illegal in most of the United States, for instance, lack of understanding is widespread and the topic is mired in controversy. On the other hand, where euthanasia has been made legal and people are more familiar with it, they see that there is nothing to fear; thus, abuse is unlikely. Marcia Angell, a senior lecturer in social medicine at Harvard University Medical School, argues that in places like Oregon and Washington, where it is legal for doctors to help patients die, it is far less controversial. According to Angell,

> A recent poll showed that 77 percent of Oregonians favor their Death With Dignity law, which permits doctors to provide terminally ill patients with medication that they may take if they choose to hasten death. The law in Oregon has been in effect for 14 years, and the evidence is clear that it is used sparingly and exactly as intended. A similar law has been in effect in Washington for three years, and is also popular.[66]

Source Notes

Overview: Euthanasia

1. Quoted in Maryclaire Dale, "Barbara Mancini Assisted Suicide Case Rallies 'Death with Dignity' Advocates," *Huffington Post*, August 18, 2013. www.huffingtonpost.com.
2. *Economist*, "Over My Dead Body: Assisted Suicide," October 20, 2012. www.economist.com.
3. Thomas R. McCormick, "Human Dignity in End-of-Life Issues: From Palliative Care to Euthanasia," in *Human Dignity in Bioethics: From Worldviews to the Public Square,* ed. Stephen Dilley and Nathan J. Palpant. New York: Routledge, 2013, p. 265.

Chapter One: Can Voluntary Euthanasia Ever Be Justified?

4. Debbie Purdy, "Should Assisted Suicide Be Legalized? Yes," *New Internationalist*, March 2012. www.newint.org.
5. Quoted in Naftali Bendavid, "For Belgium's Tormented Souls, Euthanasia-Made-Easy Beckons," *Wall Street Journal*, June 14, 2013. www.wsj.com.
6. Timothy E. Quill, "Physicians Should 'Assist in Suicide' When It Is Appropriate," *Journal of Law, Medicine & Ethics*, Spring 2012, p. 59.
7. Netherlands Ministry of Foreign Affairs, "FAQ: Euthanasia 2010: The Termination of Life on Request and Assisted Suicide (Review Procedures) Act in Practice," 2010. www.government.nl.
8. Richard N. Côté, *In Search of Gentle Death: The Fight for the Right to Die with Dignity*. Mt. Pleasant, SC: Corinthian, 2012, p. xi.
9. Quoted in Ken MacQueen, "On the Need to Restart the Debate on Assisted Suicide: Lee Carter and Hollis Johnson Discuss Death and Chocolate in a Swiss Clinic; Lee Carter and Hollis Johnson in Conversation with Ken McQueen," *Maclean's*, August 17, 2011. www.macleans.ca.

10. Quoted in the Debate.org blog, "Do Family Members of Terminal Patients Have a Higher Approval Rating for Euthanasia than the General Public?" www.debate.org.

11. Margaret Somerville, "What Would We Lose by Legalizing Euthanasia?," *Australian Broadcasting Corporation*, May 24, 2013. www.abc.net.au.

12. National Catholic Bioethics Center, "A Catholic Guide to End-of-Life Decisions." www.ncbcenter.org.

13. Patrick Lee, "Say No to Physician Assisted Suicide," *Cato Unbound*, December 2012. www.cato-unbound.org.

14. Wesley J. Smith, "Euthanasia 'Choice' Would Often Not Be," *National Review*, March 24, 2011. www.nationalreview.com.

15. Ben Mattlin, "Suicide by Choice? Not So Fast," *New York Times*, October 31, 2012. www.nytimes.com.

16. Ira Byock, "Physician-Assisted Suicide Is Not Progressive," *Atlantic*, October 25, 2012. www.theatlantic.com.

17. Americans United for Life, "Defending Life 2013," 2013. www.aul.org.

Chapter Two: Can Involuntary Euthanasia Ever Be Justified?

18. Quoted in Matt Lauer, "Michael Schiavo's Side of the Story," *Dateline NBC*, March 27, 2006. www.nbcnews.com.

19. Kristen McConnell, "End of the Line in the ICU," *Health Care Blog*, November 16, 2012. http://thehealthcareblog.com.

20. Bryan Cones, "Persistent Vegetative State? Ariel Sharon's 6-Year Coma and the Ethics of Sustaining Life," *Ethic of Life* [blog], *U.S. Catholic*, January 29, 2013. www.uscatholic.org.

21. Quoted in Lisa M. Krieger, "The Cost of Dying: Simple Act of Feeding Poses Painful Choices," *Mercury News*, November 2, 2012. www.mercurynews.com.

22. Quoted in Krieger, "The Cost of Dying."

23. Government of the Netherlands, "Euthanasia and Newborn Infants." www.government.nl.

24. Peter Singer, "The Case for Allowing Euthanasia of Severely Handicapped Infants," Big Think, August 12, 2010. http://bigthink.com.

25. Quoted in OregonLive.com, "Former Vancouver Football Player Making 'Amazing' Progress After Head Injury," December 6, 2012. www.oregonlive.com.

26. Quoted in Ryan Grenoble, "Scott Routley, Canadian Patient in 'Vegetative' State, Answers 'Yes" and 'No" Questions Via fMRI Machine," *Huffington Post*, November 14, 2012. www.huffingtonpost.com.

27. Paul Donovan, "Why Euthanasia Must Never Be the Answer to Dementia," *Between the Lines* (blog), February 21, 2010. http://paulf donovan.blogspot.com.

28. Donovan, "Why Euthanasia Must Never Be the Answer to Dementia."

29. Joseph Tham, "The Ethics of Infanticide: Why Should the Baby Die?," Biltrix, March 28, 2012. http://biltrix.com.

30. Quoted in Tham, "The Ethics of Infanticide."

31. Frank Pavone, "Reflections on Euthanasia and Assisted Suicide," Priests for Life. www.priestsforlife.org.

32. Patients Rights Council, "Questions and Answers about 'Artificial Feeding.'" www.patientsrightscouncil.org.

Chapter Three: Should Physician-Assisted Suicide Be Legal?

33. Quoted in Sanjay Gupta, "Kevorkian: 'I Have No Regrets,'" CNN, June 14, 2010. www.cnn.com.

34. Nikola Biller-Andorno, "Physician-Assisted Suicide Should Be Permitted," *New England Journal of Medicine*, April 11, 2013. www .nejm.org.

35. Netherlands Ministry of Foreign Affairs, "FAQ."

36. Quill, "Physicians Should 'Assist in Suicide' When It Is Appropriate."

37. Janice Lynch Schuster, letter to the editor, "Sunday Dialogue: Choosing How We Die," *New York Times*, March 30, 2013. www.nytimes .com.

38. Becky Proctor, "It's Time," Death with Dignity National Center, August 13, 2013. www.deathwithdignity.org.

39. Proctor, "It's Time."

40. Quill, "Physicians Should 'Assist in Suicide' When It Is Appropriate."

41. Quill, "Physicians Should 'Assist in Suicide' When It Is Appropriate."

42. J. Donald Boudreau and Margaret A. Somerville, "Physician-Assisted Suicide Should Not Be Permitted," *New England Journal of Medicine*, April 11, 2013. www.nejm.org.

43. American Medical Association, "Opinion 2.21—Euthanasia," June 1996. www.ama-assn.org.

44. World Medical Association, "WMA Resolution on Euthanasia," April 2013. www.wma.net.

45. Chris Lancelot, "Opinion: Assisted Suicide Law Must Include an Opt-Out," GP Online, July 7, 2011. www.gponline.com.

46. Center to Advance Palliative Care and the National Palliative Care Research Center, "America's Care of Serious Illness: A State-by-State Report Card on Access to Palliative Care in Our Nation's Hospitals," 2011. http://reportcard.capc.org.

47. Ilora Finlay and Debbie Purdy, "Should Assisted Suicide Be Legalized?: No," *New Internationalist*, March 1, 2012. www.newint.org.

48. Kerry Pound, "Column: A Physician's Perspective on Question 2," *Salem News*, October 30, 2012. www.salemnews.com.

49. Jeanette Hall, letter to the editor, "Assisted Suicide Prompts Some Terminally Ill Patients to Give Up on Life Prematurely," *Ravalli Republic* (MT), November 28, 2012. www.ravallirepublic.com.

50. Ezekiel J. Emanuel, "Four Myths About Doctor-Assisted Suicide," *Opinionator* (blog) *New York Times,* October 27, 2012. www.nytimes.com.

Chapter Four: Does Allowing Euthanasia Lead to Abuse?

51. European Institute of Bioethics, "Euthanasia in Belgium: 10 Years On," April 2012. www.ieb-eib.org.

52. Wesley J. Smith, "Dutch Docs to Expand Definition of 'Suffering' for Euthanasia to Include 'Loneliness' and Finances," *National Right to Life News Today*, October 18, 2011. www.nationalrighttolifenews.org.

53. Quoted in Tom Heneghan, "France Aims to Allow Euthanasia Despite Ethics Doubts," Reuters, July 1, 2013. http://uk.reuters.com.

54. Tom Mortier, "How My Mother Died," MercatorNet, February 4, 2013. www.mercatornet.com.

55. William J. Peace, "Comfort Care as a Denial of Personhood," *Hastings Center Report*, April 27, 2012. http://onlinelibrary.wiley.com.

56. Peace, "Comfort Care as a Denial of Personhood."

57. Marilyn Golden, "Another View: Assisted Suicide Fraught with Consequences," *Sacramento Bee*, July 14, 2013. www.sacbee.com.

58. Golden, "Another View."

59. Dominic Wilkinson and Julian Savulescu, "Should We Allow Organ Donation Euthanasia? Alternatives for Maximizing the Number and Quality of Organs for Transplantation," *Bioethics*, January 2012. http://onlinelibrary.wiley.com.

60. Wesley J. Smith, "At the Bottom of the Slippery Slope: Where Euthanasia Meets Organ Harvesting," *Weekly Standard Magazine* (Washington, DC), July 4, 2011. www.economist.com.

61. Bregje D. Onwuteaka-Philipsen et al. "Trends in End-Of-Life Practices Before and After the Enactment of the Euthanasia Law in the Netherlands from 1990 to 2010: A Repeated Cross-Sectional Survey," *Lancet*, July 11, 2012. www.thelancet.com.

62. Netherlands Ministry of Foreign Affairs, "FAQ."

63. Gail Van Norman, "The Ethics of Ending Life: Euthanasia and Assisted Suicide, Part 2," *CSA Bulletin*, Spring 2012. www.csahq.org.

64. Emanuel, "Four Myths About Doctor-Assisted Suicide."

65. David Benatar, "A Legal Right to Die: Responding to Slippery Slope and Abuse Arguments," *Current Oncology*, vol. 18, no. 5, 2011. www.current-oncology.com.

66. Marcia Angell, "Comfort and Familiarity," *New York Times*, June 14, 2012. www.nytimes.com.

Euthanasia Facts

Euthanasia and Assisted Suicide in Europe

- According to a 2012 report in the *Lancet*, in 2010 about 3 percent of all deaths in the Netherlands were the result of euthanasia or assisted suicide, compared to 2.8 percent before the practice was legalized there.
- The *Telegraph* in London reports that 1,432 cases of euthanasia occurred in Belgium in 2010.
- Statistics Netherlands reports that of 3,859 total cases of euthanasia in the Netherlands in 2010, 1,324 occurred among people aged seventeen to sixty-five.
- In 2012 BBC News reported that more than 180 British people have traveled to Switzerland for assisted suicide.
- According to a 2010 report by the regional euthanasia review committees of the Netherlands, between 2009 and 2010 the number of euthanasia cases reported to the committees rose by 19 percent.
- Swissinfo, a branch of the Swiss Broadcasting Corporation, reports that in 2011 Dignitas—one of the nation's leading assisted-suicide organizations—helped 144 people end their lives, and Exit—the Swiss branch of an international organization—helped 416 die.

Assisted Suicide in the United States

- The Washington State Department of Health reports that 73 percent of the people who died in 2012 under the state's assisted suicide law had cancer.
- The Oregon Public Health Division reports that the median age for the deaths that occurred in 2012 was sixty-nine years.
- According to the Oregon Public Health Division, since that state's Death with Dignity Act was passed in 1997, 1,050 people have obtained lethal prescriptions and 673 have used the prescriptions to die.

- In 2012 a Massachusetts ballot proposal to legalize physician-assisted suicide for the terminally ill was defeated, 51 percent to 49 percent.
- According to the Washington State Department of Health, of those people who died by assisted suicide in 2012, thirty-nine had known their doctor for a year or more, and forty-eight had known their doctor for twenty-four weeks or less.

Public Opinion

- In a 2011 survey of 1,018 adults, Gallup found that 45 percent believe doctor-assisted suicide is morally acceptable, and 48 percent believe it is morally wrong.
- In a 2013 poll of 2,008 adult Canadians, the Environics Research Group reports that 63 percent of respondents would support a law allowing doctors to assist patients in committing assisted suicide, and only 32 percent oppose it.
- According to a 2010 survey of 2,340 adults by Harris Interactive, 67 percent believe doctors should be allowed to advise terminally ill patients who request alternatives to medical treatment and/or ways to end their lives.
- Exit International reports that when a 2011 referendum was held in Switzerland, 78 percent of people voted that foreigners should continue to be eligible for assisted suicide there.

End-of-Life Care

- According to a 2011 report by the CAPC and the NPCRC, currently only about 1,568 US hospitals—out of a total of 2,489—offer some type of palliative care program.
- The Oregon Public Health Division reports that 97 percent of those people who died under that state's Death with Dignity Act in 2012 were enrolled in hospice.
- In a 2012 review of euthanasia in Belgium, the European Institute of Bioethics reports that in 2010 and 2011 only 10 percent of the medical

practitioners receiving euthanasia requests had been trained in palliative care.

- According to a 2012 report by the Robert Powell Center for Medical Ethics, twenty-two US states have no laws to protect patients and families who want to continue food, fluids, or life support when health-care providers decide such care should be stopped because it is futile.
- The American Association for Retired People reports that almost one-third of Americans aged sixty-five and older have had aggressive surgery in the last year of their lives.

Related Organizations and Websites

American Life League (ALL)
PO Box 1350
Stafford, VA 22555
phone: (540) 659-4171 • fax: (540) 659-2586
website: www.all.org

ALL is opposed to euthanasia. It believes that every human life is sacred and should be protected. Its website contains information about euthanasia.

Dignity in Dying
181 Oxford St.
London, UK W1D 2JT
phone: 44 020 7479 7730
website: www.dignityindying.org.uk • email: info@dignityindying.org.uk

Dignity in Dying believes that everyone has the right to a dignified death, and this means having control over how they die. It campaigns to change laws so that assisted death is legal for terminally ill, mentally competent adults who meet strict safeguards and feel their suffering has become unbearable. Its website contains information about assisted dying and many personal stories.

Euthanasia Prevention Coalition
PO Box 25033
London, ON Canada N6C 6A8
phone: (519) 439-3348
website: www.epcc.ca • email: info@epcc.ca

The Euthanasia Prevention Coalition is a Canadian organization that believes that euthanasia and assisted suicide are murder and should be prohibited. It works to educate the public about the dangers of euthanasia and to promote alternatives, such as improved hospice and palliative care.

Euthanasia Research and Guidance Organization (ERGO)
24829 Norris Ln.
Junction City, OR 97448-9559
phone: (541) 998-1873
website: www.finalexit.org • email: ergo@efn.org

ERGO was founded in 1993 to provide research and information for dying people who wish to end their suffering. It believes euthanasia and PAS are both appropriate, depending on medical circumstances. Its website contains information about euthanasia laws and numerous essays about euthanasia.

Hastings Center
21 Malcolm Gordon Rd.
Garrison, NY 10524
phone: (845) 424-4040-4125
website: www.thehastingscenter.org • email: mail@thehastingscenter.org

Founded in 1969, the Hastings Center is a nonpartisan, nonprofit bioethics research institute. Its researchers address ethical issues in health, medicine, and the environment. Its website includes information about euthanasia.

National Hospice and Palliative Care Organization (NHPCO)
1731 King St., Suite 100
Alexandria, VA 22314
phone: (703) 837-1500 • fax: (703) 837-1233
website: www.nhpco.org • email: nhpco_info@nhpco.org

The NHPCO represents hospice and palliative care programs and professionals in the United States. It is committed to improving end-of-life care and expanding access to hospice care for Americans, thus improving the quality of life for dying people and their loved ones.

National Right to Life Committee
512 10th St. NW
Washington, DC 20004
phone: (202) 626-8800
website: www.nrlc.org • email: NRLC@nrlc.org

The National Right to Life Committee is opposed to euthanasia. Its website has information about euthanasia, assisted suicide, and death by dehydration and starvation.

Patients Rights Council
PO Box 760
Steubenville, OH 43952
phone: (740) 282-3810
website: www.patientsrightscouncil.org

The Patients Rights Council believes that everybody has the right to be well informed about end-of-life decisions. Its website provides information about euthanasia and proposed laws and court cases in order to help educate society.

For Further Research

Books

Richard N. Côté, *In Search of Gentle Death: The Fight for the Right to Die with Dignity*. Mt. Pleasant, SC: Corinthian, 2012.

Emily Jackson and John Keown, *Debating Euthanasia*. Portland: Hart, 2012.

Robert Orfali, *Death with Dignity: The Case for Legalizing Physician-Assisted Dying and Euthanasia*. Minneapolis: Mill City, 2011.

L.W. Sumner, *Assisted Death: A Study in Ethics and Law*. Oxford, UK: Oxford University Press, 2011.

Periodicals

Bregje D. Onwuteaka-Philipsen et al. "Trends in End-of-Life Practices Before and After the Enactment of the Euthanasia Law in the Netherlands from 1990 to 2010: A Repeated Cross-Sectional Survey," *Lancet*, July 11, 2012.

José Pereira, "Legalizing Euthanasia or Assisted Suicide: The Illusion of Safeguards and Controls," *Current Oncology*, vol. 18, no. 2, 2011.

Timothy E. Quill, "Physicians Should 'Assist in Suicide' When It Is Appropriate," *Journal of Law, Medicine & Ethics*, Spring 2012.

Internet Sources

Americans for Life, "Defending Life 2013," 2013. www.aul.org/defending-life-2013-contents.

Howard Ball, Philip Nitschke, and Patrick Lee, "The Last Choice: Death and Dignity in the United States," *Cato Unbound*, December 2012. www.cato-unbound.org/issues/december-2012/last-choice-death-dignity-united-states.

Ira Byock, "Physician-Assisted Suicide Is Not Progressive," *Atlantic*, October 25, 2012. www.theatlantic.com/health/archive/2012/physician -assisted-suicide-is-not-progressive/264091.

Ezekiel J. Emanuel, "Four Myths About Doctor-Assisted Suicide," *New York Times*, October 27, 2012. http://opinionator.blogs.nytimes .com/2012/10/27/four-myths-about-doctor-assited-suicide/?_r=0.

European Institute of Bioethics, "Euthanasia in Belgium: 10 Years On," April 2012. www.ieb-eib.org/fr/pdf/20121208-dossier-euthanasia-in-bel gium-10-years.pdf.

Ben Mattlin, "Suicide by Choice? Not So Fast," *New York Times*, October 31, 2012. www.nytimes.com/2012/11/01/opinion/suicide-by-choice -not-so-fast.html.

Netherlands Ministry of Foreign Affairs, "FAQ: Euthanasia 2010: The Termination of Life on Request and Assisted Suicide (Review Proce-dures) Act in Practice," 2010. www.patientsrightscouncil.org/site/wp -content/uploads/2012/03/Netherlands_Ministry_of_Justice_FAQ_Eu thanasia_2010.pdf.

Gail Van Norman, "The Ethics of Ending Life: Euthanasia and Assisted Suicide, Part 2," *CSA Bulletin*, 2012. www.csahq.org/pdf/bulletin/eth ics_61_2.pdf.

Index

About the Author

Andrea C. Nakaya, a native of New Zealand, holds a bachelor of arts degree in English and a master's degree in communications from San Diego State University. She has written and edited numerous books on current issues. She currently lives in Encinitas, California, with her husband and their two children, Natalie and Shane.